QUESTIONS AND ANSWERS ABOUT

ANIMAL WORLD

Contents

Monkeys

Monkeys belong to the group of mammals called primates, which also includes apes and humans. All three species share certain characteristics, such as narrow noses and five fingers and toes. However, unlike apes and humans, many monkeys have tails. Monkeys from Asia and Africa have noses that point downward, while monkeys from Central and South America have broad noses and nostrils that open sideways.

Quick Q's:

1. Why is the Japanese macaque also known as the snow monkey?

The Japanese macaque, commonly known as the snow monkey, is one of the few primate species that live in cold regions. They are found in the mountains of Honshu in Japan. When it is very cold, these monkeys move near hot springs to keep themselves warm.

2. What is grooming?

Monkeys and apes groom each other's fur using their hands. This helps not only to get rid of parasites and dirt but is also an important part of socializing.

3. Why are monkeys called social animals?

Most species of monkeys live in groups. The size of a group depends on how much food is available and if there are predators around.

4. Do howler monkeys howl?

Howler monkeys make a peculiar barking sound. They can be heard up to 3 kilometers (1.9 miles) away.

Q What are the common characteristics of primates?

A All primates have a large brain, and their eyes face forward, allowing binocular vision. Most of them have thumbs on both hands and feet that can be used for grasping. Their highly developed brain helps them to remember things, and to understand others.

Q How many primate species are there in the world?

A There are more than 350 species of primates in the world, divided into two groups. Small to medium-sized primates, such as lemurs and lorises, have long whiskers and well-developed senses of smell and hearing. The rest of the primates, including humans, apes and other monkeys, are part of the "humanlike" category. This group consists of about 175 species. Most of these primates have flat faces and a poor sense of smell.

◀ **Big hug**
Snow monkeys are often found huddling near hot springs to keep warm.

▲ **Top of the forest**
Colobus monkeys are usually found at the top layer of branches in African rainforests.

Q What does a monkey eat?

A Most monkeys will eat whatever they come across, including birds' eggs, fruit and the sap from plants. Several species of monkey will even attack and eat other monkeys. Howler monkeys of South America and colobus monkeys of Africa eat the leaves of any type of tree. The digestive system of leaf-eating monkeys is similar to that of other herbivores, like deer and cows.

◀ **Ringed tail**
Lemurs are easily identified by their ringed tails.

Q Why are spider monkeys so called?

A A spider monkey is a species of New World monkey (from the American continent) that has long, slender, spidery limbs. It displays great acrobatic skills, using its hands and strong tail to grip branches as it swings through the trees. Spider monkeys only travel on particular routes through trees, marking the branches with their own individual scent as they go.

Q What is a tarsier?

A Tarsiers are very different from other monkeys. They have enormous eyes, long feet and are active at night. Tarsiers eat insects, but also prey on small birds, lizards and snakes. They use their long back legs to leap on to prey. Holding the prey with their hands, they kill it with their sharp, pointed teeth.

▲ **Five hands?**
The spider monkey of central and South America has a tail whose tip is so well developed it can almost be considered a fifth hand. Each tip even has its own unique "fingerprint."

◀ **Night hunter**
Tarsiers have huge eyes that help them to find prey in the dark.

Alarm calls

Monkeys use several methods of communication. A few species of monkey that live alone use scent to communicate. Urine, faeces or special scent glands are used to mark territory or to let other monkeys know they are ready to mate. Monkeys that live in groups communicate using signs and calls. Some species, like the African vervet monkeys, use different alarm calls for each of their main predators—eagles, leopards and snakes. The monkeys react differently to each call. When they hear the eagle alarm call, the monkeys hide among dense vegetation. At the sound of the leopard call they climb as high as possible.

Big Cats

A big cat is a cat that can roar! This group includes the lion, tiger, jaguar and leopard. They have large eyes, sharp teeth, excellent hearing and powerful limbs with sharp claws. Most have long tails and coats that are either striped or spotted. Big cats are found in all continents except Australia and Antarctica.

Quick Q's:

1. What do cats use their tongues for?

A cat's tongue is rough and covered with sharp, hooklike projections called papillae. Cats use their tongues to clean the flesh from the bones of their prey and to groom themselves.

2. How does a jaguar kill its prey?

The jaguar uses its powerful jaws and sharp teeth to pierce the skull of its prey between the ears. Its strong teeth can even break open turtle shells.

3. Are white tigers albinos?

White tigers are not albinos. A true albino would not have stripes, but white tigers have prominent stripes. They are not a separate species, but differently colored members of the same species. Their color is caused by a mutation in their genes, which rarely occurs naturally. In recent times, the first pair of white tigers was found in a forest in central India. Since then, most white tigers we know of have been bred in captivity and so can usually be seen only in zoos.

Q How are big cats different from other cats?

A Big cats are similar to our pet cats in many ways. However, only big cats can roar. This is because of a difference in the structure of a bone that is present in the mouth of all cats. This bone, called the hyoid bone, connects the tongue to the roof of the mouth. In small cats, the hyoid is hard, while in big cats the hyoid is flexible, helping them open their mouths really wide and roar aloud.

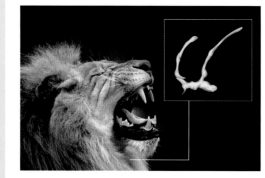

▲ **Roaring apparatus**
The flexible hyoid bone of the big cats allows them to roar.

▼ **Living in a pride**
Lions are the only big cats that live in prides. Each pride has one adult male with three or four lionesses and their cubs. Male cubs are thrown out of the pride as soon as they become semi-adults.

Q Is the cheetah a big cat?

A The cheetah is not actually a big cat as it cannot roar, but purrs like our domestic cat. However, it has many other characteristics of a big cat, and is sometimes regarded as the smallest member of the big cat family. It is the fastest of all land animals, and can run at a speed of up to 110 kilometers per hour (70 miles per hour) over a short distance.

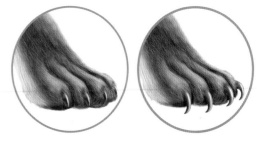

▲ **Hidden weapons**
Big cats usually draw their claws into the paw (left) and extend the claws (right) when about to jump on their prey.

Q What is special about the claws of a big cat?

A All big cats—except the cheetah—have retractable claws. These claws can be drawn into the paw when the cat is not using them. This prevents the cat from getting hurt while grooming. The cheetah has short claws. It uses them to get a good grip on the ground while chasing its prey at high speeds.

Q Why do the eyes of a big cat glow in the night?

A The eyes of a big cat—or any other cat, for that matter—have a mirrorlike tissue in them that gathers even the faintest light and focuses it on an object, making it clearly visible to the cat. It is this mirrorlike structure that causes the cat's eyes to glow in the dark.

Q Are black panthers also big cats?

A Black panthers are actually black leopards or jaguars. They are the result of a condition called melanism that is common among jaguars and leopards. This is when the black pigment called melanin in the root of the fur is produced in large quantities. It is this condition that gives black panthers their color. A few leopards and jaguars have less melanin than average. This gives them a grayish color, and they are often known as white leopards or white jaguars.

Q Are teeth important to big cats?

A Big cats rely on their teeth to kill prey. They have strong jaws, with three pairs of incisor teeth, one pair of canines, two or three pairs of premolars, and one pair of molars. Apart from jaguars, all the other big cats drive their large powerful canines into the neck of their prey, between the gaps in the backbone. The teeth cut through the spinal cord, often killing the prey instantly. The small but sharp incisor teeth located between the canines help the cat scrape meat off the bones. The molars help to crack the bones open when the cat is feeding. Jaguars usually attack their prey on top of the skull, piercing it in between the ears. They can do this because they have wider jaws than those of other big cats.

▶ **Black panthers**
Black panthers are actually leopards or jaguars with more than the usual amount of melanin.

Q How do big cats mark their territory?

A All big cats are highly territorial—each individual has a particular territory that includes hunting grounds, dens and water holes. Big cats do not like to share their territories, even with members of their own species. They warn other cats off by marking these territories, usually by spraying urine or scratching trees. Sometimes, big cats rub their cheeks against rocks, trees or any other object. Other cats usually leave the area once they smell or see the signs.

◀ **Solitary hunter**
Adult leopards usually live by themselves except during the mating season. But they require a smaller territory than a tiger or a pride of lions.

Mixing breeds

A "liger" is born to a male lion and a female tiger. This hybrid big cat looks like a lion with stripes. Some ligers have manes, while all ligers love to swim—just like tigers. Ligers can grow to be giants. Some of them even reach a height of about 4 meters (12 feet) and weigh over 400 kilograms (900 pounds). "Tigons," which are born to a male tiger and a lioness, do not grow as big.

Seabirds

Birds that spend most of their time at sea are called seabirds. These include skuas, gulls, terns, auks, penguins, pelicans, petrels, gannets and cormorants. The earliest seabirds had teeth and lived in the Cretaceous period, which began 146 million years ago. Modern seabirds have been around since the Palaeogene period that began 65 million years ago.

▲ Drying up
After fishing, cormorants have to spread out their wings to dry as they do not have waterproof feathers.

Quick Q's:

1. Are most seabirds white?

Seabirds are white, gray or black. These colors help them hide from enemies and also from prey. Their legs and beaks are sometimes brightly colored.

2. How do seabirds catch their food?

The albatross feeds on fish and krill that are found on the surface of the water. Gannets and boobies dive to pick up prey. Some, like the chinstrap penguin, dive and chase their prey. Skuas and frigate birds are known to steal food from others.

3. Is so much salt good for birds?

Seabirds have salt glands on their face that excrete some of the salt they take in. But the salt does not seem to harm the birds—seabirds live longer than other types of birds. In fact, the albatross can live for up to 60 years.

Q Do seabirds ever live on land?

A Seabirds come on to land to lay their eggs. The snow petrel nests 483 kilometers (300 miles) away from the sea on the Antarctic continent. Although seabirds usually fly and fish alone, most of them nest in colonies on land. The colonies house anything from a few dozen to more than a million birds. Murres build their nests close to each other for protection, while albatrosses prefer to leave space between their nests.

▶ Good divers
Murres dive beneath the surface to feed on fish.

Q How are seabirds different from other kinds of birds?

A Seabirds have adapted to life around saltwater. Birds like the albatross that fly long distances over the open ocean have long, strong wings to help them glide, while birds that dive for fish have shorter wings. All seabirds have webbed feet so that they can skim the water's surface or dive down in to the water with ease. Seabirds have lots of feathers that are packed densely, to keep out the water. A thick layer of down keeps them warm.

◀ Strange nest
Petrels make their nests with pebbles. They move to land only to breed.

▶ Good dads
Unlike most birds, the male phalarope guards his eggs until they hatch.

Q How far does a seabird migrate?

A Seabirds migrate a long way to lay eggs. The Arctic tern holds the record for flying longer distances than any other bird. When it is summer in the northern hemisphere, it flies up to the Arctic. And when it is summer in the southern hemisphere, it flies all the way to Antarctica. The terns travel 20,000 kilometers (12,000 miles) each way! Other long distance flyers include sooty shearwaters, albatrosses and phalaropes. While many seabirds fly over the open sea, many are happy to keep close to the shore.

Q What kind of parents do seabirds make?

A Seabirds make good parents. They nest at safe spots and are careful with their eggs. Both the mother and father care for their young. Some seabirds care for their young for six months, while some, like frigate birds, watch their young for fourteen months.

Birds of Prey

Birds of prey (raptors) are meat-eating birds that use their beaks and claws to hunt. There are about 500 species of birds of prey. The largest of them is the male Andean condor, and the elf owl is the smallest.

large, forward-facing eyes

soft, round wing edges for slow flying

▲ **Night vision**
Owls can see and hear well at night.

Q Which birds are raptors?

A Vultures, hawks, eagles, kites, falcons, harriers, buzzards, owls, secretary birds and ospreys are all types of birds of prey. Of these, only owls hunt at night. Female raptors that feed on live prey are often larger than the males, although male and female vultures are the same size. Vultures feed on carrion, or dead animals, instead of live prey.

Q What makes raptors such good hunters?

A Raptors have larger eyes than most other birds and have excellent color vision. They have a sharp, curved beak and strong feet with powerful claws (talons). Raptors' sharp ears can hear prey moving and detect how far away it is.

That's really high!

Did you know that a Ruppell's griffon vulture can fly as high as 11,000 meters (37,000 feet)? On 29 November 1973, one of these birds crashed into an aircraft over the Ivory Coast!

Q Do birds of prey have special wings?

A Falcons have thin, pointed wings. These help them to fly fast, and to change their direction while chasing their prey. Their wings also enable the falcons to dive suddenly to catch their prey. Hawks and eagles have rounded wings that help them soar, without flapping their wings, high up on air currents. They are able to mark their prey even from high up in the air.

Q What do raptors eat?

A All raptors are meat-eaters. Some, like eagles, feed on rodents, snakes, lizards and fish. Most vultures feed on carrion. Vultures have a sensitive sense of taste, so they are able to detect if food is poisonous. Some vultures, like the palm nut vulture, eat the fruit and husks of certain palm trees as well as shellfish and carrion. Bat hawks, unsurprisingly, exist on a diet of bats.

Q What is a raptor's gizzard?

A A gizzard is a specially adapted stomach that helps a bird to grind food. Birds often have stones inside their gizzards. Birds of prey have a special gizzard, which makes pellets out of whatever the bird cannot digest, like hair, bones and feathers. When it has finished eating, the bird spits the pellets out.

▲ **Majestic birds**
Eagles are larger than most other raptors, and they are more powerfully built. Their large pupils give them good night vision.

▲ **Bald and beautiful**
Vultures do not have feathers on their heads and necks. This ensures that they do not get too dirty when they stick their heads into carcasses, which helps to prevent infection.

Sharks and Rays

Sharks, skates and rays all have the same ancestors and are among the oldest fish on Earth. They were here even before the dinosaurs! These fish have cartilage or tough tissue instead of bones, and they breathe through gill slits. They don't have scales; instead their skin is covered with small tooth-shaped growths called denticles. The denticles give these fish a rough, sandpapery texture if rubbed the wrong way.

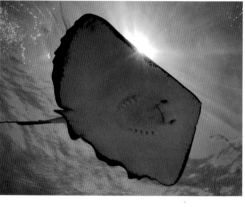

▲ Ouch, what a stinger!
The sting ray has a sharp stinger on its tail. When attacked it lifts its tail and stings its enemy.

Quick Q's:

1. Which is the earliest shark we know of?

The cladoselache is the earliest sharklike fish we know of. It grew to over 2 meters (6.5 feet) in length. It lived during the Devonian period, well before the age of the dinosaurs.

2. Are all sharks aggressive?

No. The horn shark, which is 1.2 meters (4 feet) long, hides under rocks during the day and comes out at night. It is a timid shark that eats only small fish and crustaceans.

3. Do sharks ever attack whales?

The cookie-cutter shark attaches itself to a whale and then bites out a bit of its flesh with its razor-sharp teeth. However, because cookie-cutter sharks are small, the whale is only slightly wounded by this.

4. How long do sharks normally live?

Sharks can live for many years. The great white shark can live up to one hundred years.

Q How big are sharks?

A There are over 350 species of shark in the ocean, and not all are large killers. Of these, less than 50 species grow longer than 2 meters (6 feet). One of the biggest sharks is the gentle whale shark, which is 15 meters (50 feet) long and eats plants and small shellfish. The smallest shark is the pygmy ribbontail catshark at just 24 centimeters (9.5 inches) long.

Q How does a shark find its prey?

A Sharks and rays have a strong sense of smell and can sense blood in the water hundreds of meters away. They usually find their prey through their sense of smell. They have a sharp sense of hearing. They also move very fast through the water. While attacking, an average shark can reach a speed of 19 kilometers per hour (12 miles per hour).

▶ Size matters
The great white shark is 3.7–3.75 meters (12–16 feet) long. The biggest great white shark on record was 7 meters (23 feet) long. These huge creatures are ferocious predators. They eat fish, rays and other sharks, as well as feeding on carrion (decaying bodies of fish and animals).

Q What is a ray?

A There are thousands of species of rays, which belong to the same family as sharks. Rays look like sharks that have been flattened out. They have flat, kitelike bodies that help them to glide through the ocean.

Q Can rays be dangerous?

A Rays come in all different sizes, and some are dangerous. The giant manta is enormous, but harmless. Other rays can sting or produce an electric shock to stun their prey and enemies. The lesser electric ray can transmit a powerful electric shock between 14 and 37 volts.

gill slits

dorsal fin

eye

mouth

pectoral fin

Q What is a ghost shark?

A The chimaera or ghost shark belongs to the same family as sharks, and its skeleton is also made of cartilage. Chimaeras have long tails, which they use to prod the muddy seabed for shellfish and other small prey. Most chimaeras have a poisonous spine on the upper part of their body that they use to defend themselves. They have three pairs of tooth plates: two pairs in their upper jaw and one pair in their lower jaw.

Q What is the difference between a chimaera and a shark?

A The chimaera is similar to the shark, but it has a bit of skin covering its gill slits called an operculum, whereas sharks do not. Most chimaeras have a poison-filled spine in front of their dorsal fins. The upper jaws of chimaeras are fused to their skulls, while those of sharks are not. Sharks have replaceable teeth, but chimaeras have permanent tooth plates. Chimaeras always hatch from eggs. The female chimaera lays large eggs in a leathery egg case, and the case lies at the bottom of the ocean for anywhere between six months and one year before the eggs hatch. Some sharks lay eggs and others give birth to live young. Sharks can lay up to 100 eggs, while those that give birth to live young have one or two young at a time.

▲ **Deadly teeth**
Sharks may have up to 3,000 teeth at one time. Various species of sharks have teeth of different shapes and sizes. This great white shark has sharp, wide, wedge-shaped and serrated teeth that allows it to catch and tear its prey.

Not quite a devil

The manta ray is the largest type of ray. It can grow to more than 5 meters (15 feet) wide. It is sometimes called the devil ray because of the horny cartilage on its head, but it has no sting and does not attack humans. These horns are actually fins that guide plankton and small fish into the mouth of the manta ray.

▼ **On the floor**
Chimaeras live on temperate ocean floors. They are related to sharks and rays.

Reptiles

The word reptile means "to creep." Reptiles are cold-blooded vertebrates (animals with a backbone). Most reptiles are covered with scales or plates to keep their skin moist. They breathe through lungs.

Quick Q's:

1. Which are the largest and the smallest reptiles?

The estuarine crocodile is more than 7 meters (23 feet) long. The smallest reptile is the British Virgin Islands gecko. It is just 18 millimeters (0.7 inches) long.

2. Can I outrun a reptile?

Tortoises may be very slow on land but some reptiles are very fast. The spiny-tailed iguana can run at 35 kilometers per hour (21 miles per hour).

3. How many eggs do reptiles lay?

Some tortoises lay only one egg in a season. Turtles lay about 150 eggs several times each season. Snakes can lay anything from three to 100 eggs, while crocodiles lay between 20–90 eggs at a time.

4. Would I find reptiles at the North and South Poles?

Most reptiles are found in warm, moist areas. Being cold-blooded, they cannot live in the freezing temperatures of the polar regions, with their long nights. Reptiles need regular sunlight to warm themselves up.

Q Why do reptiles like the sunshine?

A Reptiles are cold-blooded animals. This means that they need to bask in the sun and warm up to get energy. Although reptiles love the sun, they can overheat, and then they have to move into the shade and cool down. If it gets too cold out, reptiles become slow and need to sleep or hibernate until the weather is warmer. Even in sub-tropical areas, many snakes hibernate right through the winter. The population of reptiles falls off as one moves to colder regions.

◀ Lizard of the Americas
The green iguana is between 1.2–1.8 meters (4–6 feet) long.

Q Where are baby reptiles born?

A Some lizards and snakes give birth to live young, but most reptiles build nests and lay eggs in them. Most reptiles are not caring parents, and they leave the nest once they have laid the eggs, though the eggs contain sufficient food for the baby reptile. Fortunately, their hatchlings are born with the ability to look after themselves, and when they hatch, they already look like adults. Some reptiles, however, do make good parents. Alligators guard their eggs and help the hatchlings when they come out.

▲ Egg talk
Snakes search for a moist, warm and safe spot to lay their eggs. Snake egg shells are soft and leathery, not hard and brittle like birds' eggs. Baby snakes are born with a tooth, which they use to break out of the eggs. They make a slit in the leathery shell with their tooth to slither out.

Q Fish are scaly. Are they reptiles?

A A reptile's scales are different to those on a fish. A reptile's scales are attached to each other, and they are actually thick skin. Fish scales, in contrast, are stuck to the top of the skin. Blood vessels run through the lower layer of a reptile's skin, but not a fish's. As they grow, reptiles regularly moult, or shed their outer layer of skin. Snakes and worm lizards shed this layer of skin in one piece. Other reptiles shed it in several smaller pieces.

Q Which was the first reptile?

A The oldest known reptile was hylonomus. It was around 25 centimeters (10 inches) long. Reptiles developed from amphibians, and the first true reptiles had a solid skull with holes only for nose, eyes and a spinal cord. These early reptiles gave rise to another line called synapsids, which had another pair of holes in their skulls behind the eyes. Synapsids developed into mammals.

Q I'm feeling cold! Am I a reptile?

A Reptiles include crocodiles, alligators, caimans, lizards, snakes, worm lizards and turtles; but not humans!

Lizards

Lizards make up the largest group of reptiles. There are over 4,300 species of lizards. They have four legs, a long tail and movable eyelids. A lizard's lower jaw is fixed to its upper jaw, while a snake's jaws are separate.

Open frill

Colorful character

Chameleons have an amazing ability—they can flush their skin with colored pigment. This helps them to take on the color of their background so they can hide from their enemies. Some chameleons can move each eye separately, so they can see two things at one time.

Q How do I know a lizard if I meet one?

A Lizards have dry, scaly skin and clawed feet. When they are in danger, many types of lizards can shed their tail to distract an enemy. A new tail grows back.

▲ **Scary frill**
The opened frill of the lizard makes it look much larger.

▲ **Multipurpose tongue**
Lizards use their tongue to catch insects for food. They also use their tongue to wipe clean their mouths and eyes.

Q What do lizards eat?

A Most lizards eat insects. Some, like the green iguana, are vegetarians. Bigger lizards, like the gila monster, eat eggs and small animals. The biggest lizards of all, the monitors, eat small animals.

Q Is that lizard wearing a bib?

A The frilled lizard of Australia has two large frilly pieces of skin on both sides of its neck. When in danger, its frill fans out around its head and measures about 30 centimeters (12 inches) in diameter.

Q Are lizards poisonous?

A The gila monster of North America and the beaded lizard of Mexico and Guatemala are poisonous. Some of the other larger lizards can bite, but they are not poisonous. The komodo dragon's bite poisons the victim's blood. Most lizards are not dangerous to humans. In fact, they help us by eating insects.

Q Which is the biggest monitor lizard?

A The fierce komodo dragon is the biggest monitor in the world. It weighs about 135 kg (300 pounds). Its mouth is full of poisonous bacteria, and when it bites, the bacteria poisons the blood of its prey, killing it.

▶ **Poisonous**
The beaded lizard found in Mexico is a venomous lizard.

▼ **Child eater**
Komodo dragons are huge and fierce. They have even been known to eat small children.

Amphibians

Amphibians live on land and in water. Of the 6,000 species of amphibians, most begin their life in water. The skin of an amphibian is thin and moist and helps the amphibian to breathe, so they need to live in moist, damp places.

Quick Q's:

1. What do frogs and toads eat?

Frogs catch live prey (mostly insects) by darting out their long, sticky tongues. The marine toad eats plants as well as other dead animals.

2. Do toads have long tongues like frogs?

Toads have shorter tongues than frogs and have to use their wide mouths to catch their prey.

3. Why do some frogs and almost all toads secrete poison?

Frogs and toads secrete poison for safety. Most poison-arrow frogs and mantella frogs are brightly colored to warn their enemies. Some harmless frogs copy this coloring to protect themselves from predators who mistake them as poisonous!

4. Can toads help out in the garden?

Frogs and toads help to keep insects in the garden under control. They eat snails and slugs, which destroy plants. They are also an important part of the food chain. Rats, foxes, crows and hedgehogs eat them.

Q How do amphibians give birth?

A Most amphibians are born in water, where the eggs are laid. Although some frogs, toads and caecilians give birth to live young that look like adults, most frogs lay eggs in a blob of jelly and most toads lay eggs in long strips of gel. Some caecilians lay eggs in burrows. Male frogs call loudly to attract females to suitable water bodies such as ponds. At the start of the mating season, frog eggs are a favorite food of other animals in the water. So frogs lay enough eggs to ensure that some survive.

▶ **Worm lookalike**
Caecilians are amphibians that look like giant earthworms or small snakes. They live hidden in the ground most of the time. Most species have smooth, dark skin. Their eyes are covered by skin for protection underground. They have two tentacles on their heads. There are 171 species of caecilians. Most of them live in hot and moist places around the world.

Q What are the changes that happen to amphibians as they grow?

A All amphibians are born from an egg and grow into a tadpole. As the tadpole grows, its eyes grow eyelids and the creature learns to see both in and out of water. But until they become adults, they spend all their time in water. Tadpoles of frogs and toads lose their tails before they move on to land and become adults.

▲ **Long tongue**
Frogs have a long tongue hinged at the front of the mouth. They flick this tongue out quickly to catch food.

Q Is it a frog or a toad?

A Frogs have longer legs than most toads, which help them to take long leaps. The hind feet of a frog are webbed, to help it swim. Toads hop around and have dry, thick, warty skin. Unlike most amphibians, toads like to live in dry places. Both frogs and toads have bulging eyes covered by a transparent piece of skin to keep their eyes moist. When frogs eat, they close their eyes and push the food down their throat.

Q Are amphibians safe to touch?

A Most toads and some salamanders secrete a poison through their skin to defend themselves against predators. Most frogs are not poisonous, although rainforest frogs like the poison-arrow frog are so poisonous that some people tip arrows with its poison to use for hunting.

▲ **Highly poisonous**
Most of the 220 species of the poison-arrow frog of Central and South America are brightly colored to scare away potential predators.

Q How big are amphibians?

A Amphibians range in size from the tiny 9.8 millimeter (0.38 inch) Brazilian gold frog to the Japanese giant salamander, which is 1.5 meters (60 inches) long and weighs 25 kilograms (55 pounds). Amphibians are found almost everywhere on Earth, even in the Arctic.

▲ **The familiar frog**
With over 5,000 species, frogs are among the most common animals in the world. They are found from the warm tropics to the cold sub-arctic regions, but most species are found in the tropical rainforests. Adult frogs are equally comfortable in land and water.

Sing a song for her

Male frogs and toads have a special pouch in their throat that helps them to croak. The sound is amplified by one or more vocal sacs, which are membranes of skin under the throat or on the corner of the mouth. Croaking loudly is a good way to attract females in the mating season. Some frogs and toads croak loudly to scare other males away and can even puff themselves out to look bigger.

Insects

Insects make up the largest group of creatures on Earth. Eight out of every ten animals are insects. There are about 925,000 species of insects. Of these, there are about 5,000 species of dragonflies, 110,000 species of bees and ants and 3,500 species of cockroaches.

Quick Q's:

1. How many insects am I standing on?

If you are in a field, there could be dozens of insects under your feet. One acre can be home to more than 400,000,000 insects. 100,000,000 collembola (springtails) can live in a square meter!

2. Can I eat an insect?

Some insects can be poisonous. However, in certain parts of the world, people do eat non-harmful insects, such as ants, crickets and grasshoppers, since they are a cheap source of protein. But they have to be cooked in a certain way before they are safe to be eaten.

3. How long have insects been around?

One insect fossil, found in Russia, dates back to more than 100 million years before the first dinosaurs. Cockroaches are also older than dinosaurs.

4. How many babies can one pair of houseflies have?

In five months, one pair of houseflies can grow into a family of 191×10^{18} if all their young live and multiply. That is 191 followed by 18 zeros!

Q What is an insect?

A Insects are arthropods—animals that have a protective cover or an exoskeleton (a skeleton outside the body). The exoskeleton supports the body and keeps the soft inner organs safe. Since the skeleton can't grow with the insect, the insect has to shed or moult the skeleton regularly, and a new one grows back. Insects are the only invertebrates (animals without backbone) that can fly. Some insects such as cockroaches and some types of ants grow wings when they are adults. All insects have six legs. Scorpions, spiders and centipedes are not insects, since they do not have six legs. True insects also have external mouths and 11 abdominal segments.

▼ Digging up the soil

Many insects, such as ants, make their homes by digging up the soil. In the process, they move the soil around and allow air to pass underground, which improves the fertility of the soil. Using chemical insecticides doesn't only kill pests, it kills these beneficial insects as well.

▼ Long jump champion
There are more than 11,000 species of grasshoppers. Some can jump 20 times the length of their own body!

Q What is an insect's body like?

A In Latin, the word insect means "cut in sections." An insect's body has three parts: a head, a thorax, and an abdomen. The head has a pair of antennae, eyes and a mouth. The head is used for eating, to feel around and to gather information. Some insects have simple eyes like ours, but most have complex eyes made up of six-sided lenses. The second part of the body, the thorax, supports the six legs and wings. The last part, the abdomen, digests the food and helps the insect breathe, since insects do not have separate noses like we do.

▶ Lady on a leaf
There are over 4,500 species of ladybirds, which are also known as ladybugs and lady beetles. They help us by eating pests.

◄ Not at prayer
The praying mantis is easily recognized by its resemblance to a leaf and the way it holds its antennae together, as if it has its hands joined in prayer.

thorax

▼ Major pest
The mosquito is one of our biggest pests. It has a painful bite, and carries the germs of major diseases like malaria.

abdomen

proboscis

Q How do insects breathe?

A Insects have spiracles (little holes) on the sides of the thorax and abdomen. Air enters through these spiracles and then breathing tubes carry the oxygen all over the body. The spiracles close when the insect is in water, ensuring that the insect doesn't drown. However, insects have to come up for air regularly when they are underwater.

Q Why do we need insects?

A There are many insects that help us. Butterflies, ants, bees and wasps pollinate flowers and help to grow new plants, including fruit trees. Insects give us honey, medicines, silk, lacquer and wax. Some beetles eat dead animals. Some insects eat other insects. Grasshoppers lay so many eggs that if all of them were to hatch, they could eat up most of our crops and plants. This does not happen because there are other insects that eat up most of the grasshopper eggs. Agricultural scientists have been breeding insects to keep pest populations under control. This is better than using chemical insecticides, which are poisonous not only for insects but also for humans. Scientists have also been using insects as an ingredient for vaccines, for example in a new trial vaccine against cervical cancer. However, there are many insects that are undoubtedly pests. Mosquitoes, bedbugs and lice drink our blood and spread diseases. Others, like the housefly and the tsetse fly, can make us ill. Locusts chew up our crops. Termites and borers eat up wooden homes and furniture.

Long and short

One of the longest insects is the stick insect, which is about 36 centimeters (14 inches) long. It belongs to the orthoptera insect family, which includes crickets, grasshoppers, praying mantids, leaf insects and cockroaches. Most stick insects are females and they can lay fertile eggs without the help of a male. When the eggs hatch, out come more females. The smallest insect of all is the fairy fly, which is 0.17 millimeters (0.007 inches) long and can fly through the eye of a needle.

This edition published in 2012 by Arcturus Publishing Limited
26/27 Bickels Yard, 151-153 Bermondsey Street,
London SE1 3HA

ISBN: 978-1-84858-160-9
CH002012US
Supplier 15, Date 0112, Print run 1709

Designers: Q2A India and Jane Hawkins
Editors: Ella Fern, Fiona Tulloch and Alex Woolf

Printed in China